STREAKERS
of
DISTINCTION

HOW THE PROS LET GO

WILLOUGHBY P. SHERIDAN

First Printing, 2017
ISBN: 978-1-5272-1274-9

Email: questions@ofdistinction.xyz

Printed by KOPA® www.kopa.eu

Dedicated to future generations.

Don't be afraid to have a bit of fun
every now and again.

Contents

A Brief History of Streaking

ON 24ᵗᴴ MAY 2006, a Nepali sherpa called Lakpa Tharke reached the summit of Mount Everest. Lakpa paused for a few moments to take in the view, asked his climbing partner to get out a camera, took off his oxygen mask and stripped. He stood totally naked, on the highest point on Earth, for three whole minutes. Based on May weather records, the wind chill was somewhere between -39°C and -52°C.

George Mallory, the first man to attempt to climb Everest, was once asked why he would attempt something so dangerous. He famously replied, "Because it's there." Like so many streakers, Lakpa might have answered in similar fashion, when standing with his willy flapping in the breeze at 8,848 metres, caring less for the *why* and more about the *why not*?

The etymology of 'streaking' is unclear. The consensus is that it derives from a notion of speed, as in 'a streak of light'. True to this theory, no streaker I interviewed loped aimlessly onto their respective stage; they galloped or skipped, the hare before the security greyhounds, accompanied by a huge grin, and in Erika Roe's case, two cigarettes. Their stages were hugely varied: from the Super Bowl with a televised audience of over 100 million people, to the World Indoor Bowls Championships in Hopton-on-Sea, with several hundred pensioners looking on, currently sponsored by *Just Retirement*.

Ever since Genesis 3:7, when Adam realised he lacked boxer shorts and grabbed the nearest fig leaf in panic, humanity has been quietly re-testing sartorial boundaries. Written in the year 1665, *The Devil's Pilgrimage in England* recounted Quakers standing naked in town squares "to promote the naked truth of the gospel", a strange marketing construct, or maybe they had just misread the part of the Bible where Jesus revealed himself to his disciples. Either way, certainly one of the earliest records of men flashing their sausages.

A hundred or so years later, on 5th July 1799, a Gentleman attempted to streak the half mile from Cornhill to Cheapside in East London, as part of a bet (of ten guineas, around £1,000 today). The streaker made it a measly 340 metres before his arrest. It was a few more metres to Poultry Compter prison, where he was lovingly housed for the night. In an era when punts on a raindrop race down a window and a man attempting to survive underwater in a sunken ship for twelve hours (both laid at London's Gentlemen's Club *White's* – and one more successful than the other) were *laissez-faire*, it was only a matter of time before wagers turned to nudity.

The US has a long history of streaking as well; this book features Americans, as well as Canadians, Brits, Kiwis and Aussies. A few years after the East London dash, George William Crump ran naked for a bet through Washington College in clear moonlight, with a view to jumping into a public fountain, something that we might now consider a bit of a cliché but certainly wasn't at the time, and as a result he was arrested and suspended for the rest of the term. The consequences of streaking did not do much to impede his career advancement, as later in life the then Congressman Crump ended up being appointed by President Jackson as chief clerk of the Pension Bureau in 1832, a position he held until his death, and a period of his life presumably somewhat less thrilling than university appeared to be.

The world was rather short on streaks from then, until the mass adoption of television and photography through the 1960s coincided with a growing desire for a distraction from the woes of the world at the time, especially in America, which created a surge in both supply and demand.

Many of the resulting photographs are instantly recognisable, some iconic. The 1974 photo of Michael O'Brien with three policemen at the rugby (one of which is interviewed in Chapter Two) was People magazine's 'Picture of the Decade', and for the purposes of the history we are writing as we go along, formed the beginning of the modern streak as the first known streaker at a major sporting event.

Shortly after Michael, Robert Opel ran nude onto the Oscars ceremony stage, appearing behind David Niven, who was welcoming Elizabeth Taylor to the stage at the time. Niven laughed it off, quipping, "Well, ladies and gentlemen, that was almost bound to happen… But isn't it fascinating to think that probably the only laugh that man will ever get in his life is by stripping off and showing his shortcomings?"

The 70s were also the moment when it was discovered that streaking was also a good way to make a point. At the University of Maine, a meeting aimed to constrain the growing number of streaks got interrupted by a naked man running around the conference room. At a library in South Carolina, a streaker stopped at the front desk to ask for a copy of *The Naked Ape* before legging it away.

Since Twickenham, there have been about fifty notable attempts at major sporting events, but not all of them qualify for this book. It turned out that the Oscars streak was almost certainly a publicity stunt

THE CHEEK OF IT ALL

to draw attention to the show, with Niven's witty comeback eventually accused of being scripted.

There have been similar instances of streaking for motives other than fun and personal liberation. Like the Oscars, these commercial breaks are mentioned only briefly here, as they distract from the simple purity of joy the other *no strings attached* streakers represent. Sander Lantinga, who joined Maria Sharapova on Centre Court, and to her consternation was left to his own devices as he performed a nude cartwheel, and Miky from Berlin (the surprise as you turned over the last page), who nominated himself to be a model for Dolce & Gabbana at the end of their spring/summer 2014 Milan Fashion Week show, are examples of all the right execution but the wrong motivations.

Similarly, in 2004 Ron Bensimhon (right) belly-flopped off the Olympic three-metre diving board wearing a blue tutu. He technically beat a $1.5 billion security operation in completing his advertisement, and later went on to conquer the World Figure Skating Championships, this time in a gold tutu. I feel their efforts are worth noting.

RON NAILED THE DIVE, BUT
LOST VALUABLE POINTS ON
THE LANDING

MARK ROBERTS FLIES OVER ONE OF THE LESSER KNOWN FENCES IN THE GRAND NATIONAL STEEPLECHASE

And that just about brings us up to date, in terms of the streakers who are not covered in the rest of the book. As for the ones that are, Mark Roberts of Chapter Two sits on the edge of our amateur criterion as a 'semi-pro', a primarily self-funded lifelong streaker who has occasionally sought help with costs (by which I mean bail bonds) at some of his more complex appearances. One of these was the Super Bowl's first streak, at Super Bowl XXXVIII, where Mark pranced on dressed as a referee, took off his kit, danced around the ball and was arrested (see overleaf) in front of two teams of rather confused players, just before Janet Jackson hit them with her own wardrobe malfunction. When Mark arrived at downtown Houston jail, police officers took a mug shot, printed it off and made him sign autographs for everyone in the station.

Like many streakers, Mark loves nothing more than giving the police a laugh. At his first streak at the Grand National, they found themselves chasing a naked man with "a small cowboy hat on, a big Mexican droopy moustache and a bum-bag". After taking "about four furlongs" to catch him, he was told by the officers that it was one of the best times they'd had on the beat. The officials' faces in the photos I've chosen for this book often say as much as the grin of the streakers themselves – a *joie de vivre*, an infectious delight in unconditional nudity, performed for no other reason to bring a bit of light relief to the world.

Before the Super Bowl, Mark said that his streak was going to be a response to "emails from the US saying what they need is a good old-fashioned laugh. So security permitting that is what I will give them." As someone who is unequivocally committed to giving people a tickle, it would be amiss not to include him on the basis of a few dollars taken here and there, and so you'll find more on Mark in Chapter Two.

I've interviewed the most prominent twelve streakers in history, all momentarily or permanently famous in their own wonderful ways. Or eleven, plus one policeman. It's a small club, comparable (only) in number, to those who have walked on the moon, and they're split into three chapters: those who simply felt a sudden urge to storm onto the field of play, those whose antics deliberately played to the crowd, and those whose own nudity was a liberation from something more personal.

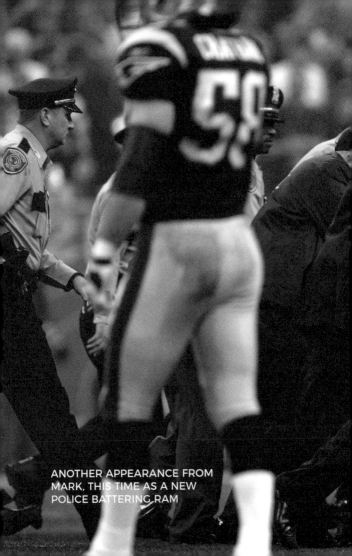

ANOTHER APPEARANCE FROM
MARK, THIS TIME AS A NEW
POLICE BATTERING RAM

In truth, there is an element of all three in every story, and an unmistakable joy that transcends their streaks. This is the theme I loved about each and every one, and my reason for writing. The following inclusions are their contributions to the history of blissful indifference, and this book is mine.

CHAPTER ONE

Missy, Lianne, Bruce and Tracy

"It can be an advantage not to overthink things"

"CARS MUST BE PARKED bonnets facing inwards", is what you have a 50% chance of being told by a receptionist if you arrive by car at Queen's Club, one of London's two historic tennis clubs. If you're the kind of person that likes a bit of structure here and there, then only six miles away you will find even more of it at the All England Lawn Tennis and Croquet Club, host of the famous Wimbledon tournament. The dress guidelines are reassuringly clear, "No solid mass of colouring. Little or no dark or bold colours.

BLISS

No fluorescent colours. Preference towards pastel colours. Preference for back of shirt to be totally white. Preference for shorts and skirts to be totally white. All other items of clothing including hats, socks and shoes to be almost entirely white." This essentially means white; and until 1986, that included the ball.

A fellow university graduate turned to Melissa 'Missy' Davis in the week leading up to the 1996 men's singles final at the Wimbledon tennis championships and told her, "You should streak." Two days later, she became the first person to run nude on to Wimbledon's Centre Court, in front of a televised audience of several million people, for no reason other than it felt like the right thing to do at the time.

Missy, Lianne, Bruce and Tracy all have their separate, historic streaks: three of them in front of millions... and then Tracy, who streaked at the World Indoor Bowls Championships in Hopton-on-Sea, bouncing down the carpet to the delight of a statin-laden crowd. Our four streakers are united in this chapter by three things: their impulsiveness, their lack of vanity and the raw delight they caused to ripple through normally 'proper' audiences.

Twenty-two-year-old Missy's extended graduation ceremony involved a job flipping posh fish and chips by day, and getting gloriously inebriated at night. "I had a bad ankle from falling off a table. I was quite wild then," she later told me. The Manchester University design graduate was schooled in a convent. "It was quite a 'feel ashamed of yourself' kind of place, quite a strange place. Nuns are not always particularly friendly. I think my streak was a kind of rebellion against that a bit." It was a kind of middle-class chaos theory; the smallest causality here leads to televised nudity over there.

Security in 1996 was rather more relaxed than now, with the ones who over-diluted the Pimm's considered the terrorists. "I gave free fish and chips to the security guards so they'd let me on the pitch near the court. I told them I was just a big fan."

After her well-plaiced bribery, Missy found herself just feet from the court. Their Royal Highnesses Prince and Princess Michael of Kent, Placido Domingo, Home Secretary Michael Howard, and the aptly named Heritage Secretary Virginia Bottomley were all in close proximity, in the intimacy

"WELL, THERE'S A PRETTY THING.
WE'VE HAD ALL SORTS OF FIRSTS THIS
YEAR. I MUST SAY I NEVER THOUGHT
I'D SEE THAT ON CENTRE COURT,"
-BBC COMMENTATOR
JOHN BARRETT MBE

of the prestigious Centre Court setting. As finalists MaliVai Washington and Richard Krajicek finished their knock up and walked to the net for a coin toss, Missy, "sober as a judge" – that's a judge who's sober but decides to strip in front of several million people on live TV – made the decision of a lifetime.

"I sat there and thought, right, well sod it, I'm going to do it, so I had this dress on that I just undid the buttons of, took it off and I had the little white pinny on underneath."

Missy Davies

The live TV coverage is wonderful. The shot is of Krajicek and Washington, seen standing professionally at the net. Krajicek notices something to his left, his face lights up, his gaze pans right, and suddenly, something fleshy flies past in the foreground. For just a second, the home audience thought they saw something, but couldn't be quite sure; Missy flashed past just long enough for millions around the world to turn to their right on the sofa and ask, "Was that what I thought it was?"

Missy remembers the 'sublime and liberating' feeling of the Wimbledon lawn underfoot, of which every shoot of each of 54 million blades of grass are trimmed a millimetre a fortnight in the exhaustive preparations the club makes in the build up to the tournament. As she trampled across the court, Missy thought, "right... what am I going to do?" She ran up to the delighted-looking players, and lifted up her apron. To her utter surprise, Washington flashed her back by lifting up his shirt. "I saw these things wobbling around and, Jeez, she smiled at me," he said afterwards.

Guests of Royal Box were seen to be laughing while Missy "sort of wiggled around there for a bit. I didn't really want to be rugby tackled by the police, so I ran towards them and they ran towards me." She was gently embraced by the police under the Royal Box, and escorted off. The crowd were still cheering and clapping minutes later, as Sir Cliff Richard, having had the wind ever so slightly taken out of his sails,

LUCKILY THE BAD ANKLE
DIDN'T PLAY UP

AT LEAST SHE'S
WEARING WHITE

stood up for a different kind of impromptu concert to the now highly distracted audience. Krajicek and Washington couldn't stop grinning.

The police "were so sweet", and gave her a police jacket, before escorting her to Wimbledon police station, where she was charged with indecent exposure. There was considerable proof to corroborate the accusation. Missy's boss from the fish and chip shop arrived, then left, being there only to retrieve the pinny which she had worn in strict, if momentary, adherence to the all-white dress code when on court. Wimbledon caterers' staff handbooks often include clauses stating bonus payments are to be awarded based on performance, and I think Missy is still genuinely surprised she failed to meet the grade.

The *Sound of Music*'s von Trapp family might have struggled with Missy's parents reaction. "We're so proud of you! We saw you!" they exclaimed when she returned from the police station, promptly throwing a barbeque in her honour. Although, when asked by the press the next day, her mother Carole did by then concede, "I'd like someone to come along and take her off my hands!" Her mother was a "sixties girl" and both parents had "quite a wild time when they were young". Missy says that her mother, who now has a picture of Missy's streak on her wall, "probably gave me *carte blanche* to be the same as her," adding, "I wouldn't be surprised if my children go through their wilder moments."

"Life seems full of absurdities and laughing in the face of it seems to me as good a way as any. Plus… I had a very nice fan club of boys at boarding school, and I got lots of clippings and letters from them which was really sweet." Joy is contagious.

APART FROM THE carefree spontaneity of their acts, Missy, along with Lianne and Tracy who follow in the pages to come, are also united by the intimacy of their chosen stages. Size of venue must inversely be more intimidating in some ways; you see the giggling whites of your audience's eyes, and are more vulnerable to being shopped when undressing. The audience-streaker relationship is more personal, the wave of joy that ripples across the chosen arena magnified.

In February 1997, Lianne Crofts found herself driving down to the snooker Masters final, featuring Steve Davis and Ronnie O'Sullivan, at the Grand Hall at Wembley Conference Centre. She hadn't told anyone except her brother, her boyfriend Steve and a friend, "in case I bottled it at the last minute".

Steve had promised he would drive her, and reassured her at the time that if it all went wrong, he would appear and take the blame. Steve reneged on both promises, neither coming with her nor taking any blame. Thanks to a lack of company from chivalrous Steve, as we will now call him, Lianne arrived at the Masters final all on her own, having got lost on the way up to London. Late, and having never watched a snooker game in her life, she crossed over into the conference centre, the only streaker in this book to go it alone.

Lianne Crofts, at 22, was a similar age to Missy. They both streaked at international finals, in a somewhat intimate setting, for bets placed in drinking establishments. As with most of the streaks in this chapter, 'Why not?' is the pervasive tone.

Working her way up through the Wembley audience, a drunken bet with fellow students seemed from another lifetime as she realised her seat was wedged into the centre of a row. She envisioned climbing, completely naked, over several middle-aged men and two old ladies to get onto the snooker arena. They might have loved it, but she didn't want to take the risk.

She feigned illness, suggesting she might have to run out of the arena at any minute, and deftly managed to swap seats with one of the old ladies at the end, who took pity on the poor girl feeling under the weather. When I spoke to her in 2016, she still remembers it vividly – sitting alone, heart pounding, watching a game she knew sod all about, with the sage advice of her brother playing through her mind, "Don't sit there thinking 'any minute, any minute' because then you'll get to the end of the match and you won't have done it." With the clock ticking, what seemed like the ideal moment presented itself.

She ran down to the edge of the arena, past David Beckham and Gary Neville who were in the audience, and planned to jump into the ring, but the barrier was "a bit higher than I thought", admitting that at five foot two, she'd find it hard to "pop over it".

"The crowd had just cheered and were being a bit raucous anyway, and the umpire said, 'Can everyone calm down and show some restraint', and I thought, I'll show him restraint, whipped off my skirt, and the lady next to me went 'Ooh!'"

Lianne Crofts

Clambering gingerly over the barrier, with the small crowd of onlookers that had originally shown sympathy to her illness now watching a very rapid recovery, Lianne finally made it into the arena, "skipped around a bit, and blew a kiss at the camera". John Street, who was the umpire for the match, and at 65 due to retire that day, thought it was a prank being played on him. Ronnie O'Sullivan covered up the speechless umpire's eyes, then comically wiped Street's brow, and a normally sedate, respectable crowd went bananas.

TA-DA

IMAGE SHOWN IS A STILL QUOTED FROM BBC TELEVISION
FOOTAGE. COPYRIGHT © BBC, 1997 (SEE NOTES)

Davis, competing for his third Masters title, in the biggest final that exists in his sport, claimed afterwards that he was concentrating so hard he only saw her back; many years later, he came clean: "Actually the young girl did me a favour." O'Sullivan had won the first two frames with a century break, but after a nude interruption, Davis came back to win the final, and the Masters title, ten frames to eight. He genuinely believes Lianne had much to do with it.

In a crowd of only 2,500 people that moment played dividends to the atmosphere, and indeed to Davis. Snooker is not darts; it's more akin to a night of Bridge with the vicar, and Lianne's nude skip across her stage was met with delightful roars.

After running from corner to corner in a kind of victory lap, she was grabbed sternly by the previously untested security guards, and taken down to an office, "where they were very disapproving". Punishment was dished out – "we won't allow you back", they harrumphed – which was absolutely ideal. "I don't like snooker but Stephen Hendry is quite cute," she later told the *Daily Express*, adding in *The Sun* that snooker needed a lift anyway, because it was "depressingly boring."

The reporters outside Lianne's house, her friends who were there to greet her, her employer fragrance business Perfect Scent, her mother Brenda, in fact almost everyone apart from her grandparents "were really cool with it… I knew Mum would be anyway." Brenda told *The Sun* the how she phoned Lianne's 86-year-old grandmother, a snooker fan watching the final on TV. "She said it was a good game but was spoiled by a silly young girl who had streaked. I had to tell her it was our Lianne."

"I didn't know anything about snooker, but I did know that a streak had never been done at it before." Lianne had completed a world first.

"HAVING STUDIED the whole unsavoury incident on forty-three occasions, including slow motion replays," a World Bowls Championship spokesperson told reporters in Hopton-on-Sea, "we have decided against implementing a rule that spectators should remain clothed at all times."

Hopton-on-Sea is a quaint little Norfolk village near the sea, which is also home to Potters Leisure Resort, established in the 1920s. Potters Leisure Resort is an Ibiza for people who prefer *Songs of Praise* over minimal techno. "The average age was fifty-five, at least that meant we didn't have to queue for the assault course," reads one *Trip Advisor* review. Extensive

WOULD BE STRANGE IF THIS WAS IN FACT THE SPORT ITSELF, AND THIS PICTURE WAS A NORMAL PHOTOGRAPH OF IT.

research shows there are three things to do here: visit the Atlas Theatre, do some pre-arranged dancing in fancy dress, and go to the annual World Indoor Bowls Championships. The World Bowls website currently reads, "Stay in the heart of the action and experience the thrill and excitement of the 2016 *Just Retirement* World Indoor Bowls Championships", an invitation to streak if ever there was one.

Bowls is normally played in complete silence and involves trying to find a good line to throw the ball and waiting for the weight of the ball to roll it into the desired location, as it comes to a halt. If you're still reading this, matches during the championship last between two and three hours each, occasionally interrupted by someone sighing.

On a grey and misty Monday morning on 18 January 2000, while the rest of the country was wondering whether the Millennium Dome was worth it or not, the World Indoor Bowls Championships was lolling into its ninth day of an exhausting seventeen in total. A very typical morning of bowls had seen more wooden balls rolling up and down the green carpet. World number one David Gourlay and his sixty-year-

"I JUST HOPED SHE'D STOP."

old Welsh opponent Les Saunders had been battling it out for the second round of the men's singles. They were about to become witness to the most exciting event in the history of bowls – probably the only exciting event in the history of bowls.

Bowls was something Tracy Mayhead, in the audience, clearly adored: "I never understood what was going on. I used to find it quite boring," she explained in *The Sun* afterwards. "So I thought I'd liven it up a bit. I was due to leave my job anyway so I had nothing to lose."

According to The Mirror, after a drink with friends, she went to the bowling green for a *reccy* on where to run out and where to hide. "I got myself prepared, a couple more drinks, and shaved my legs in case someone tackled me."

Selflessly not wanting to go on mid-play and put the players off their game, though she probably achieved that anyway, Tracy hid behind a display stand. A friend from work signalled to her when the bowlers were at the other end of the green. "As soon as she waved me on, I pulled off my fleece, tracksuit bottoms and trainers… and ran. I was like 'Whoosh' across the green!"

> "I was going to strip off but keep my trainers on. I told some of the guests what I was going to do and they told me to take them off. One of them said, 'Oh, you can't wear trainers on the green. You'll get in real trouble.'"
>
> Tracy Mayhead

Cheered on by 500 spectators who suddenly had a reason to live, Tracy flew down the full 40 metres of the rink and planted a kiss on both players. "There were a few gasps but they cheered and clapped." Streaking had arrived at bowls with a bang and the crowd loved it.

Both players seemed to be equally bowled over, with Saunders, who was appearing in his first world championship, later telling the *Eastern Daily Press* (the

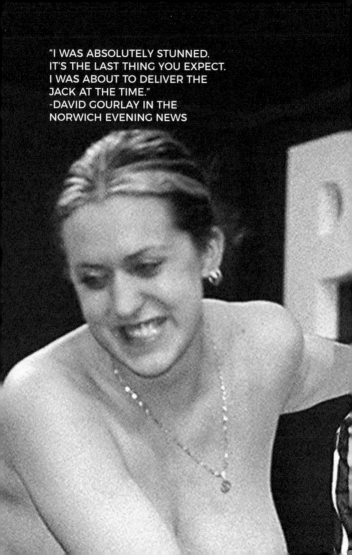

"I WAS ABSOLUTELY STUNNED.
IT'S THE LAST THING YOU EXPECT.
I WAS ABOUT TO DELIVER THE
JACK AT THE TIME."
-DAVID GOURLAY IN THE
NORWICH EVENING NEWS

New York Times of Norfolk), "I just couldn't believe it. I wondered what the hell was going on… I was looking for David for guidance, David being the world number one – but I didn't get any." In doing so, he also got a glimpse of what it meant to be a World Indoor Bowls Champion. David Gourlay went on to win the match, but not the singles championship, however, he did pick up a title win in the pairs, which I'm sure readers of this book know.

"Tracy is quite classy" her father told the *Sunday Mirror*. "I was shocked when I opened the paper and saw her. I recognised her face – although not the rest of her." Which may have been a rich statement, given kettle Tracy says black pot Roger had a reputation for "streaking around the warehouse" when celebrating Christmas at work.

"The next day I was splashed all over *The Sun*, which was a bit embarrassing. God knows what got into me. I just wish I hadn't tried to vault over the barrier because I fell over and then had to climb over slowly, one leg after the other… revealing more than I'd intended. I looked so wobbly." She told the *Sunday Mirror*, "Bits do tend to fly." Despite "some of the press being pretty bad because obviously I 'wasn't a small girl'", Tracy, now forty, doesn't have any regrets. "You don't have to be tiny to have a bit of fun."

At the time, her hopes of being a children's TV presenter may have suffered a little set back, but did she receive bouquets from strangers, calls from admirers and "a little old lady even came up to me and gave me the thumbs up."

Potters also received a dose of viagra. An elderly guest was reported to have told Managing Director, John Potter, "That's the best £4 I have ever spent, and I'm definitely coming back."

"Tickets for this weekend are sold out. I hope people realise now that we bowlers have fun as well."

Bowls spokeswoman
Anne Dunwoodie

A FORMIDABLE OPPONENT,
ESPECIALLY IF YOU'RE A STREAKER

KIWI BRUCE MCCAULEY, twenty-six, was the only streaker in this book who was apprehended *au naturel* by one of the sportsmen on the field of play. Australian cricket captain Greg Chappell had previous form in taking streakers to task. Having attempted a citizen's arrest during a match, he gave a warning that he would deal with any further malarkey seriously. He blamed Michael Angelow (who appears in Chapter Two) for the glut of nudists scuffing his crease; and that of his brother Ian's, who is one of the bowlers in the famous picture of Michael hurdling the wicket at Lord's Cricket Ground.

At Eden Park in Auckland, during Australia's second test during their tour of New Zealand in February 1977, Bruce, in what he described to me as "merely a spur of the moment decision", essentially picked the wrong guy to meet in his birthday suit.

"Likely fuelled by alcohol", cheered on by the 20,000 strong crowd, wearing nothing but headphones round his neck, and holding his arms aloft in the air, Bruce headed straight for batsman Greg Chappell. As if testing his will, he went for a handshake on reaching him. The wicket rapidly got stickier as

Chappell, clearly agitated by the *third* streaker that day, grabbed Bruce's hand and spanked him five times, hard, with his bat. "I don't know what I was thinking at the time," regrets Bruce, "There was no consideration given to risk in the slightest,"

"I didn't know if he was going to try and souvenir a bail or some stumps," Chappell later mused in a documentary. "I had my bat in my left hand and gave him a couple of sharp cracks across the buttocks just to try and get him to stand still."

"I did have the last laugh as he was run out (for fifty-eight) the next ball, which he said was due to loss of concentration!" reflects Bruce. In the video footage it's hard to see whether Chappell reached the crease. It is possible that the umpire was inclined to give Chappell a taste of the kind of ruthlessness he had dispensed to the pitch invader moments before. In any case, we will never know, but Australia went on to win the match anyway by ten wickets. Bruce was charged with disorderly conduct, fined NZ$25 and earned the nickname the 'beaten streaker'.

THAT'S A CRICKET BAT
NOT A MEASURING ROD
ORPHANED PHOTO
ORIGINALLY PUBLISHED
IN MIRROR SPORT,
28 FEBRUARY 1977
(SEE NOTES)

MISSY DAVIS RECEIVED a lifetime ban from Wimbledon after her streak in 1996, while in a day for career firsts, Richard Krajicek went from saying, "I never dreamed of playing Centre Court" on the BBC while waiting for the rain to clear beforehand, to becoming the first unseeded player to win the title since Boris Becker in 1985. Well-heeled nakedness appeared to go down so well that just a month after her appearance at Wimbledon, another streaker with an extensive pearl earring collection ran on to the Lord's ground carrying a hat all the way, during the first test match between England and Pakistan, much to the amusement of the chaps in the background of the picture on page 50.

Despite being hidden away in a hotel by News International, in order to keep her out of reach of competitor newspapers, and suffering an unwelcome "chase round the bedroom" by a senior journalist, Missy was not through with streaking (but she was through with interviews, giving nothing further away until our conversations). Not long after the Wimbledon streak, Missy's boss decided she "should go to a typography convention", where Missy showed her displeasure by defiantly taking off her clothes, despite it being "really embarrassing because there were only about thirty people there… and they were all chin strokers". One senses this was a kind of test imposed on herself. Her third and final nude appearance was at an Iggy Pop concert where she "got thoroughly over-excited and as they were pulling people on stage, I got up there, took off my clothes, and licked the end of Iggy's guitar during 'The Passenger'. I had to be dragged off."

"It makes me laugh to think of doing it again at the same place. To be honest I'm not sure anyone would like to see me naked now… there was an article on my fat ankles. But I think keeping a sense of humour goes a long way."

Missy Davies

Lianne became a driving instructor, albeit one that may have been heavily reliant on sat nav, and probably the first driving instructor to have done

QUITE POSSIBLY THE MOST
GENTRIFIED STREAKING
PHOTO EVER

anything particularly risky at all. As for the referee, John Street told *The Sun* that Lianne's streak caused him to have "second thoughts" about retirement.

For Lianne, life is about experiences, and creating lasting memories. "I did a topless bungee jump for charity when I was eighteen, a few years before my streak, to raise a bit for Comic Relief, and I went on to do several more bungee jumps." Losing oneself in the moment is an art form to the streakers in this chapter. They react to situations that need their input the most, but even they have limits. I asked Lianne if she'd do another streak now. "No! I'm a responsible mother."

"In some ways I'm quite old fashioned when it comes to drugs, relationships, sex. I've always been really anti-drugs, I just found fun in other ways. I don't need to get high to get high, instead I like to find other ways to be mad."

Lianne Crofts

Bruce reflected to me while holidaying in Fiji that his streak "occurred thirty-nine years ago, and is something I thought would be well and truly dead and buried, but it raises its head every so often". Having been spanked hard by Greg Chappell in front of several thousand people, Bruce had a successful career "in the credit and finance industry... For the last thirty-odd years I have always resisted making myself available for ridicule over this event." He added, mischievously, "However, I have recently entered the retirement stage of my life." Greg Chappell went on to become a prominent figure in both careers of cricket and willow wielding, deftly using the bat and a firm grip on the streaker, in an Australia vs West Indies match in Melbourne, in 1979, to cover the streaker's crown jewels until the authorities arrived.

In her moment on the lawn, Tracy said she "didn't feel naked", and all she was conscious of was the cheers from the crowd. In Tracy's streak, Bowls found its mojo. World Indoor Bowls champion David Gourlay later said to the documentary Streakers, "Bowling was talked in in circles it had never been mentioned in before. Tracy did us all a big favour.

It was something we all needed and it came at the right time."

Shortly after perfectly capturing the spirit of irreverence in her streak, Tracy got a job at the Stakis Hotel in Maidstone, Kent. At the time her father Roger said to reporters, "I just hope she doesn't develop a taste for it and start whipping off her clothes when she's serving guests." Tracy now works in Sainsbury's, with her clothes on. She misses her holidays at Potters Leisure Resort but advises, "Don't go during January."

When I interviewed Missy about her Wimbledon streak, in 2016, she mentioned she'd gone for a job interview shortly after her streak. The job was in a shop called Magnificent. It was run by Dan Macmillan, the great-grandson of former Prime Minister Harold Macmillan.

Dan looked at her CV, and portfolio, up and down. He then asked, "Did you streak at Wimbledon?!" Nervously, she replied in the affirmative. He replied, "OK. You've got the job." Missy has worked for him ever since.

BAT MEETS BALL. GREG CHAPPELL
ON THE RUN AGAIN IN 1979 DURING
THE AUSTRALIA V WEST INDIES ONE-
DAY INTERNATIONAL, AT THE MC

CHAPTER TWO

Michael, Mark, Michael and Tim

"It's very important to put on a show, and entertain the crowd as much as possible."

THE GROUND UNDER Michael Angelow's feet was technically a wicket, but for Michael it might as well have been a meadow.

England were playing Australia at Lord's on a sunny 4 August 1975, in the Ashes, heading for a draw on the fourth day. The heat was extraordinary for London – 33°C. Twenty-four-year-old Michael sat in the stands, wallowing with some Aussies in a few beers. A little back-n-forthing ensued and before you could say *owzat*, Michael had been bet he couldn't

IN A FIELD OF HIS OWN

run across the pitch, in just a pair of black socks and Adidas trainers.

The heroes in Chapter One found themselves in a collision of time and place that told them in no uncertain terms, that a bit of light relief was needed. This happens to everyone, every day, but they reacted to it in their own magnificent style. Michael is symptomatic of the altogether different beast of Chapter Two: one that sets out to play to the crowd.

In a display of good sportsmanship he waited until the end of Lillee's over, before making his move. "It was a hot day and I had my top off anyway, like a lot of people did there, so it was just a case of dropping the jeans and underwear." Our heroes in this chapter plan little, deliver a lot.

As Michael raced on, BBC commentator John Arlott struggled to find the right words, so new to modern sport was streaking: "We have a freaker on the wicket now! Not very shapely," adding disappointedly, "and it's masculine."

Having found his crowd, Michael galloped from the Tavern End to the middle of the pitch, leapt like a young fawn in spring over the first set of stumps, flew down the pitch, leapt the at the second set like a hurdler, and finished up at the Nursery End with a victorious wave of the fist. As well he might: he had just become Britain's first cricket streaker.

England's Alan Knott was batting at one end. "A couple of Aussies said something. Alan Knott was just laughing too much to say a word," Angelow recalled.

As he reached the Nursery End, Michael realised 25,000 people were cheering wildly. "After I cleared the second set of stumps, it was just like being in a goldfish bowl, there was nowhere to go, that's what I remember most. I didn't realise the impact it was going to have."

"I would think it's seen the last of its cricket for the day," broadcasted John Arlott. "The police are mustered, so are the cameramen, and Chappell... and now he's being embraced by a blond policeman... He's now being marched down in the final exhibition past at least 8,000 people in the Mound Stand, some of whom perhaps have never seen anything quite like this before. And he's getting a very good reception..."

A FINE MIDDLE WICKET

Richie Benaud, also in the commentary box, put it more delicately with understatement and obfuscation seemingly the reserve of 1970s newsreaders: "There was a slight interruption there for athletics."

> "Fine performance but what *will* they do about finding his swimming trunks?"
>
> BBC Commentator
> John Arlott

Michael was arrested by the bobbies at Long Leg, taken to the local 'nick', processed and landed in Marylebone Magistrates Court the next morning. The magistrates and police found the novelty of streaking highly amusing. Asked how much the bet was for, Michael said £20. Magistrate Lieutenant-Colonel Bill Haswell, in a bit of tit-for-tat streakonomics, promptly removed the same £20 from him before finishing solemnly, "Please moderate your behaviour in the future." Michael Angelow was sent away, the man who

TAKE THAT
HAND AWAY
FROM YOUR
TROUSERS

changed the number of security guards at the cricket forever.

Michael, now sixty-five, loves the sport of it all. I remember the day with deep fondness, he says, while keeping me up to date with live scores of Murray vs Kyrgios at Wimbledon, "The best bit? Beforehand with the fans. It was such a good day." The streak, for Michael as it was for Mark (who's up next), will always be secondary to the game. That's probably why he and his fifteen-year-old brother Lawrence went straight back to watch the match the next day, where, looking as suspicious as a pub with a flat roof, he unconvincingly explained to the *Daily Express*, "I do not intend to take anything off today, no matter how hot it gets."

In the Wisden obituary for the umpire Tom Spencer, who can be seen in the pictures enjoying himself very much at the sharp end of the wicket, photographer Patrick Eagar is said to have given the legendary stump-hurdle photograph to him as a retirement gift. Spencer was said to show it from time to time at Seaton Delaval working men's club. There is arguably no better photograph in cricket. The image of Michael Angelow's hurdle will endure far beyond the many English and Australian newspapers that summer, as well as the cover art of the Duckworth Lewis Method's second album *Sticky Wickets* that followed.

A few months afterwards Eric Morecambe and Ernie Wise featured the streak in their Christmas special, in a sketch that saw Eric play the role of Michael. Those few months could have been particularly busy for Michael given the newspaper attention. But as a Merchant Navy chef, he was mercifully at sea only two weeks later. "I escaped, basically." This drew a neat line under all streaking for him. That, and refusing several serious offers to star in a porn film.

I'VE GOT A BETTER CV than any athlete on the planet. I've reached every final of every major sport," announces Mark Roberts, a claim that on inspection of his glorious record is fully justified. I interviewed him in 2016; he was just back from the Rio Olympics, "where a soldier pulled a gun on me as I was trying to streak the 100-metre final".

STRIKING A
BUM NOTE

I suspect readers of this book will not have looked into streaking as a full-time career option. With no discernible motive other than to "give people a laugh", painter and decorator Mark has devoted a lifetime to performing streaks, generously self-funding his efforts to get his knob out on over 500 occasions.

He joins Missy in having streaked the tennis at Wimbledon, and he's streaked the dog show Crufts (where he donned a cat-shaped mask over his own *dachshund* to protect his modesty). He's streaked the Miss World and Mr Universe competitions, and run nude with the bulls in Pamplona. On a live broadcast of *This Morning* in 1995, he swam onto presenter Fred Talbot's floating weather map and proceeded to copy Talbot's trademark leap from Scotland to Ireland, though rather less successfully. Mark is as close to a professional as you can get.

It all started in 1993, when he found himself in Hong Kong watching the infamous annual Rugby Sevens. A female streaker had run onto the pitch the day before. Mark bet his friends in the stands he could do the same; later he put this down to "ale talk".

The next day, his friends "were kicking down the door. I was asleep on the couch in last night's clothes. They grabbed me, threw me in a taxi and drove me straight back to the Rugby Sevens. I didn't even know what day it was. They took me straight up to the bar. The first pint made me feel worse. The second levelled me out a little bit. The third I was just about OK. So then I took in the stadium. It was a carnival, everyone was having a party, different from a football match in the UK, and I felt the buzz and thought *sod it, I'm going to do it.*"

Mark ran down through the main stand, stripped and hit the pitch. As the New Zealand All Blacks and the South African Springboks lined up to start the game, Mark picked up the ball, deliberated, then ran the entire length of the pitch to score a try.

This was Mark's first appearance in the nude at a major event. "It was the moment that changed my life. The buzz was that great." It was also the first of many goals scored at matches such as the Liverpool vs Chelsea Carling Cup game at Anfield in 2000, where he took a pass from Gianfranco Zola, defeated the entire Chelsea defence, before drilling it past the keeper.

He maintains a strong code of ethics. "Never be offensive, never approach anybody, and never interrupt the progress of the game. Take off your clothes once you are visible, so they know where to get them to bring you the clothes afterwards. Don't eat curry the night before."

That code served him well for two particular streaks, a daring dash at the Open and a flying leap at the Ryder Cup. In July 1995, at the Open championship at St Andrews, Scotland, John Daly had just putted his last ball on the eighteenth hole to win his first Open championship and second major title in a four-hole playoff over Costantino Rocca. Mark waited for Daly's final putt, before running on nude. "His wife beat me," reflects Mark, as at precisely the same time, John Daly's wife Paulette came onto the green to give her husband a celebratory hug. Mark had to instead exit stage left pursued by security. In photographs of the streak, over the page, you will see a number of police officers in hot pursuit, which Mark describes as "the cast of *Benny Hill*", who you almost expect to break into a "'Allo 'allo 'allo, what 'ave we got 'ere?"

If you look a little closer, you also see what looks like an erstwhile member of the public giving chase alongside them. "I looked behind me and there was a policeman chasing me, but there was also Fred." Fred was a canny Scotsman, who had struck up an unlikely rapport with Mark after attempting to charge him £5 to enter a free car park the day before. He'd heard what Mark was going to do, and wanted to get in on the action. "Fred asked, 'Can I chase you?' so I said, 'Yes, you can chase me but don't try and catch me.'" Fred was a value-adding employee.

President George W. Bush and HRH The Duke of York were in close proximity as a naked Liverpudlian, dressed only in a cloth cap he discovered "in an allotment in Maidenhead", with '19th Hole 6' written in permanent marker on his back, launched onto the green, followed by a parking attendant.

ARGUABLY THE MOST PRIMEVAL
JOY IN THE WORLD; RUNNING
NAKED WHILST BEING CHASED BY A
HIGHER AUTHORITY. IN THIS CASE,
FRED FROM THE CAR PARK.

GREAT WORK FRED

> "Everybody loves to laugh, no matter where you're from, what class, what job, everyone loves a laugh."
>
> Mark Roberts

Mark heard Fred plead, "Slow down, I'm having a heart attack here", shortly before he was rugby tackled to the ground by the wily car park attendant, and was then taken to the police station. A sheriff fined Mark £250. The police couldn't stop laughing.

Mark considers there to be three main aspects to a successful streak: timing, the show and then the chase. "I think the chase is the best part to watch as I like to try to outrun and dodge for as long as possible, making my pursuers look daft." In his Open dash, Mark achieved all three.

The way Mark describes his rituals in the morning of a major event like the Ryder Cup, you might mistake him for one of the athletes he will meet later in the day.

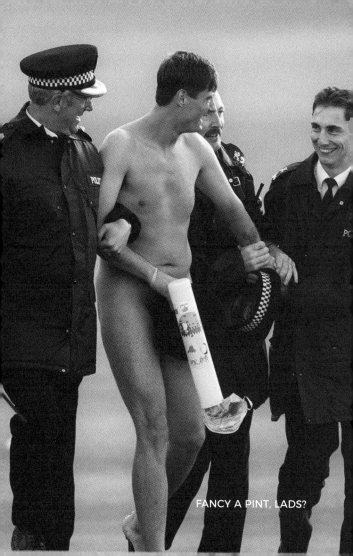

FANCY A PINT, LADS?

> "I go into my own world, I don't want to speak to anybody, I make sure everything's planned properly in my head. It's intense. Stomach's going to bits. Heart's pounding. Mind is racing."
>
> Mark Roberts

Mark plans his performances in meticulous detail, often up to a year in advance. "I have to think on my feet" both before and during the streak.

Despite meticulous planning, streaks are still fraught with risk. At the 2006 Ryder Cup at the K Club in County Kildare, west of Dublin. Mark was hiding behind a TV camera stand, in a crowd five deep. "I saw two balls come over, and was waiting for one more", but he couldn't see for sure, so shouted to some other bewildered spectators, "Is it over?"

They confirmed it was, and so he proceeded to "strip me clothes off, jump over the path security, over a stream, and onto the green". But something was wrong. Play had not finished, instead the American was just lining up his putt. "You could have heard a pin drop." Mark later called his too-early entry the "biggest mistake of my career".

Mark's found himself standing on the green wearing nothing but a wig strapped round his waist to shield his *Herman von Longschlongenstein* from view, whispering, "I'm so sorry" to one bemused world class golfer by his side and the other, lining up the putt, at waist level.

Suddenly Mark saw two Irish Guards coming over; security not to be trifled with. "I thought, *sod this*", and, reacting on his feet, ran across the green and did a flying belly flop into the lake, as the two golfers shook hands in the foreground, oblivious to the splendour behind them.

Mark is now engaged to Suzi after a two-year relationship in which she's "held his clothes" three times. "She absolutely loves it." Mark has three children. 'My two youngest, I've been doing it since before they were born. They grew up with it, didn't realise till teenagers what was going on. At that point they were like, 'Dad, come on, what are you doing?', so I went 'OK I'll slow down a bit.' I had gotten to

THE BBC RAN A CAPTION COMPETITION FOR THIS PHOTO. THE WINNER WAS SUPPLIED BY JON BALL: "THE RYDER CUP HAD SUPPLIED SPORT'S MOST BIZARRE SIGHT EVER, MCGINLEY AND HENRY INNOCENTLY SHAKING HANDS WHILST SUPERMAN AND THE INVISIBLE WOMAN MADE LOVE IN THE BACKGROUND."

a point I could do three, four, five major events in a year. My grandchildren will hopefully see me for who I am. Someone who made people laugh and was a decent man. I'm not a normal 9-5 guy," he says, with some understatement.

> "Life's for living and I love entertaining people even though I'm fifty-one now, and as long as I can entertain people I see no reason to hang up my boots."
>
> Mark Roberts

SOME PEOPLE DO OVER 500 STREAKS. Some do one, and set themselves up to fail spectacularly. This chapter has been about people who set out to captivate an audience. Nothing speaks to a crowd more than witnessing a fellow who knows that they will almost certainly fail, giving it a go anyway. Eddie The Eagle's ski jump, despite being 20 lbs heavier than the nearest competitor and needing to wear thick glasses under his goggles, which fogged up at altitude at the Calgary Olympics in 1988 stands as the best example and guardian of the great principle that it's the taking part that counts.

On 17 October 2002, Timothy Hurlbut, a twenty-one-year-old student studying professional golf management at Lethbridge Community College in southern Alberta, Canada, clambered tenuously into that group, by becoming the first of only a few people to have ever attempted to scale the steep perspex wall and streak across an ice rink.

The match in question was held in Calgary's Pengrowth Saddledome, as part of the National Hockey League, between the Calgary Flames and the Boston Bruins. Timothy was sitting in the 'nose-bleed' seats right up top, and was dared $200 to clamber over the ice rink wall by a friend. "I was at school working nights at Walmart from 11pm at night to 7am in the morning. I went to school from 9am in the morning till 5pm in the afternoon. I'd sleep for a couple of hours and then do it all over again. That's how you have to pay your way through school, and I needed some new textbooks." For reference, this is not a defence that works in a Canadian court.

"Streaking's funny no matter what, it adds an element of surprise to something. A streaker on ice is just really funny,"

Timothy Hurlbut

During a 'stoppage in play' with just five minutes to go, and with the misfortune, or luck, depending on how you look at it, of coinciding with 'a TV time-out', Hurlbut stripped. He claims it "only took three seconds to get my clothes off". His streak was even shorter.

The regulation NHL glass wall presents something of a sporting challenge in its own right. Summoning the courage of a prison break, an athleticism that saw limbs flailing all over the place, and with only red socks and a wrist-watch for grip,

Timothy began his ascent. The view from the top must have been quite something for both Timothy, and nearby spectators, to behold. If you want to get a feeling for what this must have been like, have a quick look at the expression on the face of the woman in the bottom right corner of this photograph:

THIS PHOTOGRAPH WAS THE SUBJECT OF A DEBATE ABOUT WHETHER IT HAD BEEN MANIPULATED BY THE PHOTOGRAPHER TO REMOVE THE STREAKER'S COUNT SCHLONGULA, WITH PHOTO EDITORS CONCLUDING IT HAD BEEN MANIPULATED (SEE NOTES). IMAGE QUOTED HERE AS IT WAS ITSELF THE SUBJECT OF NEWS.

At the top of the glass barrier, however, Tim's foray, rather than just beginning, was just about to end. "Not sure if I tripped or if someone grabbed my foot, but the last thing I remember was a guy in the penalty box reaching for me." Approaching a terminal velocity to make lead balloons jealous, Tim fell "from the top to the bottom", landing off-balance on the -9ºC hard ice onto his head, knocking himself out cold.

"That was kinda the downfall." After a delay of about five minutes lying motionless on his back beside the boards, he was taken to the waiting police at the side of the rink. Timothy awoke shortly after to hear the audience booing the police's presence. "So I gave a 'rock on' sign" and the boos turned into a 15,000-person standing ovation.

"I really had no plan," Tim later reflected. "Maybe steal a puck and a stick, and go shoot at the goal with it."

Asked afterwards by TSN in Canada if he thought it was a Boston fan, Joe Thornton, who assisted on the three Boston goals, replied, "I don't think so, he had red socks on. You guys can have him."

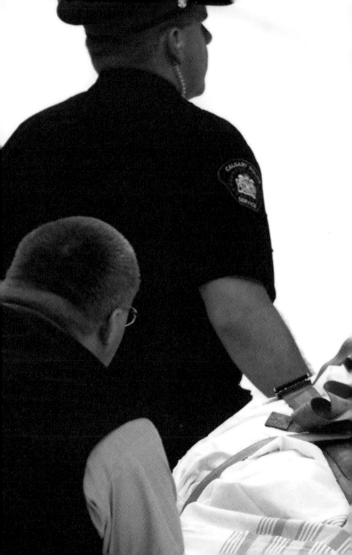

GIVING THE CROWD A "ROCK ON" FINGER SALUTE, NAKED, ARRESTED, AND ON A STRETCHER

"The whole of Provost is going to know now. I mean, my church group – I am a born-again Christian and this is not going to help," Tim's mother Jackie told reporters from the Canadian Press the next day, adding that she couldn't wait for the whole affair to "blow over". "I worried about him for just one moment, before I wanted to kill him."

Facing five years in jail, Tim hired an attorney who bartered his streak down to remove the criminal charges, but include thirty-five hours' community service. Judge Cheryl Daniel was reported in the Globe and Mail as referring to the "pathetic spectacle of yourself splayed naked on the ice for six minutes until you were covered", and ordered Tim to donate

$1,650 to charity. "I was going to be up 200 bucks, but it kind of backfired on me," Hurlbut said. "Now I really can't afford those books."

Despite spending only 0.3 conscious seconds on the ice before spontaneously combusting, ten years later Tim would find out that he'd actually laid the foundations for the historic accomplishment he had begun, to be completed – and this came in the form of twenty-three-year-old Christian Langford-Snape.

To be fair to Tim, Christian could not claim to be a streaker since the British army officer emerged onto the very same rink wearing boxer shorts; but to be fair to Christian, neither could Tim because unless you were the lady in the bottom right of the corner of the photo on page 88, you would have seen more stretcher than streaker. Neither set the world on fire, but together they made the first foray onto ice in the history of streaking.

"I heard about Tim five minutes before my own streak" recounts Christian, who at the time was fresh back from a military tour in Afghanistan, living in Banff for a few months. "All I knew was he didn't get very far before slipping and knocking himself out

SKATING ON THIN ICE
COPYRIGHT © DARREN
MAKOWICHUK/CALGARY SUN/QMI
AGENCY, 2013. (SEE NOTES)

on the ice. I knew I would be the first to streak the same Calgary rink since his attempt ten years ago, so as long as I stayed conscious for longer than ten seconds, I would pretty much beat him." He would have, by 9.7 seconds.

"Without anybody else seemingly willing, I thought it was my turn to step up to the plate."

Christian Langford-Snape

The glass wall, now three foot higher since Tim's escapades, towered above Christian. Under heightened security, rink ushers now paced up and down the aisles and stood by the court entrances, intercepting running nudists like Pac-Men.

"I had climbed over a lot of walls in the army, so I didn't think I would have too much of a problem." On the third attempt Christian managed to get his hands to reach the top of the wall, with what he describes as a "running ninja jump" – a technical term for a jump over an ice hockey wall.

Christian still has no idea how he landed on his feet, but he was now free to begin the long waddle towards the middle of the rink. "I was not going anywhere fast, but I felt free to march across until the staff clocked on to me. Once I was in, there was no getting out." He had one objective: to reach the ice hockey goal, "hoping the buzzer would sound once I crawled in there".

Unfortunately for everyone, he never made it that far. Two security officers on ice skates headed straight for him and, potentially, his toes.

"The difference between keeping my boxers on and taking them off was a plane ticket back to the UK. As much as I would have liked to go full nude, I think I made the right choice."

Christian was escorted off the premises and released with a year's ban from the stadium and a $172 fine. All of this turns out to be wonderfully out of character for him. "I am actually pretty boring. I will not ride a roller-coaster or bungee jump, because accidents happen." In this case, "I knew it was just a bit of harmless fun, I just thought *sod it.*"

MICHAEL O'BRIEN WILL forever be remembered as the person who gave meaning to the design of policemen's helmets, and for the messianic photo which became *People* magazine's 'Picture of the Decade', *LIFE* magazine's 'Picture of the Year', and won a World Press Photo award, such was the novelty of a streaker in 1974, and his captor's reaction to it. The best bit about the scene, if you look at it from another angle on the next page, are the faces in the crowd.

PRIZE IF YOU CAN SPOT
ANYONE UNAMUSED

Worldwide fame after the now notorious England v France Rugby Union match wasn't short lived, which has proved a bit of a thorn in the side for Melbourne-based stockbroker Michael. In 1991, an Australian underwear brand called Holeproof used it in an advertisement, where a caption had Michael asking the policeman, "Excuse me, officer, is this the way to the 20% off underwear sale?". In 1995 it was used in the UK to advise that phone numbers were having a digit added.

Constable Bruce Perry, the policeman holding the hat in the photo, remembers the day with clarity. "At Twickenham rugby club it was a really lovely atmosphere, and in those days we used to walk around the car parks and the ground, because we were taught to have discussions with punters."

"I spotted a group of Australians drinking Fosters; in those days I didn't even know what a Fosters was. You don't say no to that kind of thing. Well, you didn't in those days… the Twickenham crowd were happy, we were chatting"; such was the conviviality and rapport between the police and the fans, that Michael and his friends then took him into their confidence.

"They said to me, 'We're going to streak', and I said, 'What?'" Unaware of the phenomenon and with the verb yet to enter British parlance, Bruce the policeman needed it explaining that, "They were going to take their clothes off and run across the pitch." Michael was effectively stating his intention to become the world's first streaker at a major sporting event.

Bruce turned to them. "For Christ's sake, don't streak anywhere near me. Don't embarrass me", because by this stage he'd "had a couple of Fosters... and things like that".

"IT WAS A COLD DAY AND HE HAD
NOTHING TO BE PROUD OF"

"You'd walk around in your 'poacher's mac', seeing the same people time and time again, lovely people, some of them with their Rolls Royces in the car park, and you might hear 'Hello officer, how are you? Would you like a chicken leg?' or 'Glass of champagne, officer?'"

Constable Bruce Perry

Bruce walked all the way round the other side of the pitch and was under the Royal Box when the Aussie made his move (by now you will be aware that Royal Boxes feature prominently in streaks). It was half-time, and Michael, sitting near the quarter line, had sent his clothes to the other side of the pitch; this was highly advanced behaviour, given that his was the first streak in the modern era.

"I recognised him," said Bruce. "The bet was to cross the pitch where I was, before running up to and touching the stand." Bruce caught the streaker, and then in a gentlemanly show of fair play, escorted him to the stand to allow him to complete the bet.

"I was so embarrassed because I went through the whole caution, and he looked at me, turned round over his shoulder, and said 'Give me a kiss.'" It was then that Bruce decided, impulsively, to cover Michael's family jewels, perfectly cupping their contents in his hat. The rest is history.

Michael was charged at Twickenham police station for "insulting behaviour", fined £10 by magistrates who "took it in good hat", the same amount of the bet he was due to win.

One of the best bits about this story, was that he was then taken back for the second half of the game "in the Panda". "Nowadays people are always having to look over their shoulder and make sure they're doing the right thing but back then you simply treated people with respect and you got back the respect you deserved," Bruce reflected. "I'm sure this happened on this occasion, no hassle from him whatsoever, and that's why we brought him straight back into the ground." Michael found himself back in the exact same seat, having become the first person to streak at a major sporting event, in history.

"He doesn't realise he was the one who started off streaking. He was ten years before Erika! I'd have needed two helmets there, obviously,"

Constable Bruce Perry

"Nowadays by the time you'd gone to the CPS and done this, that and the other you'd have been there till kingdom come. It was the way you dealt with things in those days. Rugby crowds were high-class yobs, but they didn't act like a football crowd. They drank but they didn't get too silly."

"I was scared back at the station that I'd be given a reprimand but it was taken in the spirit it was intended. I did get calls from quite senior officers; none were negative, all were saying 'Well done, Bruce.'"

The following day Bruce found reporters standing outside his house and thought, *What the bloody hell are they talking about?* "My sister who lived in Aylesbury at the time said, 'Do you know you're on the front page of the *Daily Mirror*?!' I didn't because we didn't have a paper delivered in those days. I bought quite a few."

As one of the starring roles in a performance that brought a smile to many people's faces around the world, Bruce recalls that the event "makes me feel very happy about it."

"After that incident at Twickenham I became more of a rounded and happy person who could see both sides of everybody's story."

Constable Bruce Perry

"You've got to be careful, but it's important not to overthink things," he reflected – almost the exact same phrasing Missy used when pondering her

INTO THE LONG ARMS OF THE LAW

Wimbledon streak sixteen years later. The ability to see the humour in situations is a quality Bruce took into his future career, after retiring from policing, as an environmental safety officer in Hammersmith. It must have been easy to forget that Bruce was the main protagonist in one of the world's most famous photos. In his new role, he had to work closely with Ken Bates, who was then chairman of Chelsea Football Club where he was responsible for ensuring building works, and other projects, complied with safety regulations, in the wake of Hillsborough.

Ken and Bruce had a love-hate relationship, often finding themselves on differing sides of an argument, such as Ken's *Jurassic Park*-style proposal to install electric fencing to deter hooligans, which was rejected in 1985. "Ken could be a right so-and-so and used to take the piss out of me. I was his enemy, so to speak, but I worked like stink for Chelsea, such as when I found an extra area leading up to the directors' gates to increase their capacity to 42,000 spectators."

As Bruce was doing his final inspection in Stamford Bridge towards the end of the season, he heard his name being called out over the loudspeaker across the stadium: "Perry! Where are you?" Bruce followed the instructions over the loudspeaker, and arrived to find the London Mayor pulling a curtain back over a plaque marked 'Perry's Passage' above a corridor. "Everyone said it was Bruce's back passage! When someone like Ken does that to you, you feel very pleased. He really loved Chelsea."

THE STREAKERS IN CHAPTER TWO were showmen. Michael Angelow, who hurdled the stumps at Lord's in just a pair of trainers and black socks, thinks of his moment simply. "It gave thousands of people a good laugh, and I'm happy with the way things turned out."

A spokesman in an MCC tie said to the Daily Express the next day, "It isn't cricket, but we were mildly amused."

Mild amusement wasn't something Michael's mother registered. "I can only think," she said gravely, "that he must have gone up to London and started drinking and as a result done this dreadful thing. He is in for a ticking off."

Commentator John Arlott forecasted that it "may be his last public appearance – but what a splendid one". Michael is keen to ensure it remains his last public appearance, and I'm sure future generations of Angelows will agree that it was certainly a splendid one.

Tim and Christian, though they have never met, have also pondered the 'why'. Timothy Hurlbut notes, wistfully, "They'll always get you in the end. They're on skates so they're faster than you" but also and somewhat more philosophically, that events like these add colour to the fabric of life, and perhaps make our careers and family lives more interesting as a result.

Fame weighed heavily on Christian. After making the front page of Canada.com and USAtoday. com, as well as being featured on TSN and NBC, his only regret was that "the photos weren't better. Pretty much anything that came up on YouTube was filmed using a potato."

> "Streakers aren't necessarily all that uncommon, but people who knock themselves out on the ice, yeah, that's a little rare,"
>
> Emergency medical services spokesman Mike Plato to Reuters after picking up Timothy.

Sentimentality for a streaking 'moment' stretches back to Twickenham, where the helmet now resides in the Twickenham Museum. Its owner, Constable Bruce Perry, has no less than four framed original cartoons drawn in the next day's papers adorning the walls of his home, with articles behind, "to give provenance to them".

His favourite part of the "lovely picture" is "that steward or official from the Rugby Union running out behind me with his coat ready".

Despite the unrelenting global attention that his lightning rod for streaking generated, the most crucial aspect of this streak has gone undiscovered. Not only did Michael O'Brien plan how he would streak and what he would do in the moment, he also planned how he would be caught, and by whom. Constable Perry claims that he was not his captor by chance; he was chosen, befriended and made a part of the plan before it was even in motion. "I was part of the bet. What you don't know is that he had planned to run across the pitch and find me." As a chronological first in the world of modern streaking, it was an incredible effort, and worthy of the streaker's highest praise.

As for Michael O'Brien, he reflected on Australian TV show "Where Are They Now?" on Channel 7 in 2006 that, "It was an Englishman who put me up to it. My Australian mates said to him straight off, 'Don't bet with O'Brien because he'll do it!' The Englishman insisted, so I said, 'Well, it's going to happen.'" He can draw comfort from the fact that it seems to have become a memory cherished by those in the Royal Box. Years later as a governor at the Richmond Adult College, Constable Bruce Perry was part of a line-up of people waiting to shake HRH Princess Alexandra's hand. When his turn came, she

HRH PRINCESS ALEXANDRA SPOTTING A
STREAKER ON ANOTHER OCCASION, AT THE EPSOM
DERBY RACES WITH HRH PRINCESS MICHAEL OF
KENT. A RARE BLEND OF POMP, PAGEANTRY AND
ENTIRELY ACCEPTABLE EXPOSURE

shook the former policeman by the hand and said, "Mr Perry, you saved me from being embarrassed on one occasion." Bruce was lost for words, and so the Princess affectionately recounted the whole episode in front of him. It seems that the apology Michael offered her in the Monday papers following his streak had not been necessary after all.

Mark Roberts, the almost-professional, managed to earn his own nickname in the Spanish media, '*El Marko*' where he has done five streaks to date. When I talked to him, he spoke of the importance of respect and originality: "You have to do something that's extraordinary." He has disdain for those who choose otherwise. Instead, he chases down the extraordinary with an infectious sense of humour, aiming to create little moments that are "silly and unexpected", such as when he ran down the stairs and tried to claim asylum under the table at the snooker Masters final in 2004, or his timing of the disruption of Anna Kournikova's Wimbledon match to coincide with the exact moment the umpire called for "New balls, please" (see front cover).

The performers in this chapter are rewarded for their originality by the simple pleasure they give their audiences. At the closing ceremony of the 1988 Winter Olympic Games, the president of the Organizing Committee singled out former plasterer Eddie the Eagle for his contribution. Frank King declared to the assembled athletes, "You have broken world records and you have established personal bests. You have captured our hearts. And some of you have even soared like an eagle." Everyone loves to see an unexpected performer soar like an eagle.

CHAPTER THREE

Erika, Sheila, Rose, and Jacqui

"Something light-hearted can stand as a beacon for something powerful"

"WHO GIVES A DAMN if I turned them on?" explains Erika Roe. "Take a deep breath, there's more to me than my dippy streak."

It had been a busy few weeks of partying for Erika. Christmas, followed by her birthday on 30th December, then New Year's Eve, and finally an invitation to see England face Australia in a Rugby Union match on January 2nd. The twenty-four year old bookshop assistant only started to feel human again after a few beers in Twickenham's famous beer tents which "undoubtedly lubricated the madness."

VERY IMPRESSIVE SIDE-BURNS

Feeling "spurred on by the glorious, electric atmosphere generated by the family". That is, the world of rugby, Erika, plus her friend Sarah Bennett, ran onto the field in what the BBC would come to describe as "probably the most famous streak ever".

> "At half-time I found myself streaking. Cigarette packet one way, bra the other way, and off I went."

> Erika Roe

Sarah found herself assuming the role of a decoy by getting quickly apprehended, leaving Erika to streak topless across the ground to 60,000 cheering fans, with a couple cigarettes in her mouth, chased by a policeman. Erika would later described the feeling on the pitch as 'knowing what it's like to be in the Rolling Stones.

Sparing the blushes of Her Majesty the Queen in the Royal Box, the arresting policeman, in what had now become something of a tradition, covered half of

Roe's chest with his helmet while leading her off the field covering the other half with a sheet of fabric.

Erika returned to catch the end of the match before heading to the local pub to recount her experiences over a few jars, during which she was overheard by a group of soldiers, officers from Sandhurst in full uniform, who must have thought they had died and gone to heaven. Cooking breakfast for at least one of them the next morning, Erika and her friends expected a short mention on the sport pages, so it must have come as something of a surprise to discover almost all national (and many international) newspapers leading with the story on the front page.

Erika still puts the ensuing media circus down to "lack of a cheerful story in the media". Her father read more into it, "I find it difficult to understand such a ballyhoo over a girl who simply has full breasts. She has a dignity of bearing which comes from carrying five-gallon cans of water in the bush, when I was running a tea estate in South Africa," her father Peter told *The Mirror*, adding, "It was a lovely picture, she had her arms out like the Pope" – presumably where

LIKE A DEAD-HEAT IN A
ZEPPELIN RACE

A 24 ¼ HAT SIZE

the similarity ended. Her mother continued, "She takes after her father's side of the family."

"After the streak, I turned down more money than I had ever earned, to pose nude. I told them to go to hell. Money is not always the master. My friends and family could not understand: "But you have just stripped topless in front of the whole world – for nothing!"

The phone rang for three years with offers such as "hotel, pub and shop openings, new businesses and rugby club dinner invitations", including a request to take over Kevin Keegan's role as a model for men's double-breasted suits for the tailoring chain Harry Fenton. "We think Erika could be the epitome of the double-breasted look," Tony Edwards, Fenton's Marketing Director, told the *Daily Express*.

Another bizarre advertisement read, "Wanted: 42-inch chested girl for half-time entertainment. No experience necessary." Struggling Doncaster rugby league club's general manager Tom Morton breathlessly updated readers a few days later, "We think we've found someone. If people are depressed, she would like to cheer them up". The saga continued with reports of "Angry feminists threatening to picket the match when Ms Anderson was set to make her debut", in a column in the *Sydney Morning Herald*, headlined "Storm in a D Cup".

Erika was brought up as the third of six siblings, all tutored at home in Tanzania by her mother. In Mrs. Roe's class, her students were liable to jump out of the window and disappear until the afternoon. When she was thirteen, the family returned to England, leaving everything behind due to the political and economic situation. Erika moved to a boarding school in Dorset. It was "a massive culture shock, and a painful separation from family".

Erika journeyed from "the glorious wilderness of Africa" to boarding school in Dorset, before working as a cabin cleaner in the twilight hours on ocean liners in Southampton with her mother to make ends meet.

> "I learned, with the help of the wonderful motley crew we worked on the ships with, that I could survive this crazy life by always being myself, and not being afraid to be the first to laugh at myself"
>
> Erika Roe

Erika Roe shared her laughter, and confidence with *the family*. "I am truly honoured to be part of the history of Twickenham rugby. I am treated with great kindness by its members, and I have made good friends there."

That spirit, so clearly evident in the story of Erika's life, was put out on display for the world in her streak. Erika prefers to describe it as an 'act'. The acts in this chapter expose something very personal to the world.

Fortitude and self-belief became hallmarks that project accross the rest of Erika's life and the trials it threw at her as she went from a bookstore in Petersfield to running an organic farm in Portugal while looking after 3 children, after her husband left her.

Her children helped Erika re-build her life, building two rustic cottages out of a ruin, 800 metres from the west coast of Portugal, for holiday lets and a third home for herself nearby after the farm was sold.

Building her life up from scratch was not easy. "I had an old bath, which I buried in the ground and filled with water in the morning. By the end of the day, because it's so hot in Portugal, it would be warm enough to have a bath. So I was bathing outside, in the dark, under the night sky." Series 3 of *The Island* with Bear Grylls, which she took part in 2016, must have been a walk in the park.

"I have lived in council houses and manor houses. I have dined with tramps and nobility. I have met superstars and lost their addresses. Most importantly, I have lived my life believing in myself. I do not live my life to impress others. Society is so hell-bent on worrying about what other people think of them. Appearance – I care not tuppence for that."

Erika Roe

SHEILA'S STREAK WAS A LIBERATION. By spring 1989, after two utterly unfulfilling years at English boarding school Felsted in Essex, 19 years old Sheila Nicholls was a ticking time bomb (albeit the harmless kind chosen by the cast of this chapter) ready to explode onto the world stage driven by something powerful and personal.

Public school had taught her very little about the world except what not to like about it. As a result she was preparing to retake her A-levels. Convinced she would fail, and concerned about disappointing her father, she travelled to London to share a flat with her first love, Ed, someone she was still "super into". On arrival, Ed announced he was dating her friend.

"I had nowhere to go, but he was retaking A-levels as well, so I went there. I had a stiff upper lip, but I was completely devastated and gutted."

A few days after moving into Ed's Kilburn flat, Sheila found herself watching the Ashes with Ed on the television. Lord's Cricket Ground was only two miles away. She kept on thinking about Erika Roe, who had streaked onto the Twickenham pitch in 1982. She remembered that look on Erika's face.

"I said, 'You know, that's what I'm going to do today.' He said, 'No you're not', and I said, 'Yeah I am', and to start with I was kind of kidding, and then I wasn't, and this strange thing happened where there was a change in the balance of power, and the more he kept saying, 'No you're not', the harder I was like, 'Yes I am.'"

Rising to his challenge to "prove it", they rode Ed's moped to Lord's, and waited outside asking people for unwanted returned tickets. "He was still saying, 'You're not going to do it', and at that point it dawned on me that there was no going back."

"I was very excited and something in me said *I have nothing to lose and I don't give a jot about this* and it was really, honestly, my first feminist action: *to hell with all of this, all of you people.* And that's what it was."

Sheila and Ed walked half way round the outside of the field. This was not for the love of the game, but because she knew the broadcast on BBC2 would be going live at 4.30pm. As the clock hit the half hour, and with six weeks to go before her exams, Sheila got up from the eighth row back where they were sitting, hurtled down the stairs, and jumped the first of two boundary boards. In the metre of grass between, she took off everything she was wearing except her watch. "I just threw everything down, and then I jumped over the next one, and just ran."

English fielders averted their gaze as Sheila danced past with a huge smile on her face, waving her hands in air. She describes the feeling of running out as a "singular, ecstatic, unusual and new place inside my being where I could hardly even feel the boundaries of my own body".

One person who did want to grasp the boundaries of her body, or rather remove her body to the boundary, was the security officer who gave chase. "I saw this bloke in the corner of my eye, starting to chase me, remember thinking *this guy is not going to get me*." To end up rugby tackled to the ground, falling over and flailing naked under a strange man was not the finale she had envisaged for her feminist action. Instead, she swerved away from him, running faster until he gave up, and then, performed a cartwheel, "which was a complete 'up yours'".

"When I got to the other side this sweet umpire grabbed me. He was very embarrassed, hid his eyes, held my shoulders, and then he put his coat on me and led me into the pavilion." Inside, the batting Australian team had formed a line to shake her hand.

OWNING THE OUTFIELD

A BONUS CARTWHEEL

"I was utterly embarrassed at that point because I hadn't really processed it all." It suddenly hit her. "While I was running, my body was engaged, but when I stopped running, I was no longer in that personal space. I realised I was at a public event and I was naked."

Once her clothes had been gathered from the field, Sheila was escorted out of Lord's via an underground tunnel, not a public exit, to escape the press, then hopped into a police car and was driven to Paddington Green station.

After a short while in a cell, Sheila was released without charge. She called her father, who she had not spoken to in five months from the station, "When I called he was very happy to hear from me. We small-talked for a while and then I finally said, 'Dad did you hear about the streaker?' He said, 'Yes, bloody funny wasn't it?' and I said, 'Where were you when it happened?' He was listening to the radio, doing some gardening. I then said, 'Dad, it was me!' It took a while for it to soak in."

Sheila was asked to return home immediately. As she stepped out of her red Fiat at 2am, she saw the press waiting outside the house.

Inside the house all was not well. Her mother and father were distraught. By 5am there were people in the back garden with zoom lenses. "We'd just moved into the house and my mother went running around putting towels up in the windows, as we didn't have curtains, so we could have privacy." At daybreak, her father told Sheila's brothers to "get every tabloid newspaper". She was in every single one.

As morning continued, slips of paper kept appearing under the door with offers of money for an exclusive interview. The offers got larger as the day progressed but the family refused to take advantage of the situation, instead agreeing to do an interview for the Associated Press for nothing.

Though she says that the episode was very distressing for her father, "and I regret that", there was a subsequent experience, a feeling: it was facing the music at home, falling back into the role she had left behind when she ran onto the pitch: that of the misbehaving child, spending hours in her bedroom the day afterwards, listening to what she had done being "defined for her" downstairs. The feeling strengthened her view that her act was, at least in part, a reaction to not having the voice and independence she felt her age warranted.

Sheila wears as a badge of honour her profile as one of the first 'commoners' to enter the Lord's pavilion. As opportunistic as it was, she claims that she would never "have done it at a soccer or rugby game". Causing men in MCC ties in the pavilion to spill their G&Ts in surprise was part of the plan.

The backdrop to her act was that of applied pressure, patriarchy and public school constraint. The unnatural school environment, the subservience she experienced in her family, the unreciprocated love for Ed; in all cases, she found herself wrestling with an imbalance of power.

> "I had learned to be deferential to the masculine, I think most girls or women do; This was a few years ago, but feminism is still the subject *du jour*."
>
> Sheila Nicholls

Lady Godiva (literal translation *God's Gift*) would have sympathised. In around the year 1030, the relation of King Harold had a bit of a domestic with her husband, the Earl Leofric of Mercia, about the punitive tax regime he was imposing on his subjects, as you do.

Without worrying himself too much about the ethics of settling a conundrum that would affect a huge number of people with a naked dare, legend has it that he finally announced he would relent if she rode starkers through the local Coventry marketplace. As genuine a streaker as any in this book, Lady Godiva casually trotted past, stripped of her fine jewellery and at a minimum her outer clothing; historians seem to agree that she was at least 'symbolically naked', much to the delight of the townsfolk and the dismay of the Earl, who reluctantly kept his word, removing all taxes save those on horses.

Sheila made a similarly irreversible, albeit slightly more personal statement, which briefly echoed across a national consciousness.

"It reminds me of how something light-hearted can stand as a beacon for something powerful, and if I feel overwhelmed or weak, I can look back on that and realise that at the drop of a hat I can do something that can become real for 24 million people."

ROSE KUPA'S ACT was a rejection of constraint. On the North Island of New Zealand some time in 2007, eighteen-year-old Rose was knocking back Jack Daniels with her friend while writing down life goals into a 'bucket list'. While her friend was slightly more circumspect, looking forward to a successful military

WHETHER THE POSITION
OF THE HAT WAS A SELF
IMPOSED ADDITIONAL
CHALLENGE IS UNCLEAR

career climbing the ranks, New Zealand Army driver Rose aimed to "ride Harleys round Route 66 in America and streak at a major sporting event".

With the slight problem of America being 7,000 miles away and no international sporting event having taken place in Napier for over ten years, Rose contented herself with two other goals based a little closer to home, one of which was buying a house, and the other was "putting my name on the other side of the gorge" opposite it. Being extremely hard to get to, Rose set out dressed in high-visibility workwear, armed with a clipboard to complete the disguise and spray paint to complete the graffiti. If you happen to be around the Bay Cities, passing a gorge with a bungalow opposite and sheep grazing around, you will see the words 'Rose Kupa' still adorn the cliffs today – one of the two indelible marks Rose has left on the world.

Seven years afterwards, the stars aligned for a chance at one of the original bucket list ideas. "I think it was the first time they'd had international teams playing in Napier, as we've only got small grounds, in twenty years. Normally I have to travel away."

Rose, 25, made her final decision five hours before the New Zealand vs Argentina rugby test match, with the determining factor being that she'd "just come off a weight loss challenge and felt pretty good". She was surprised to find her two younger sisters "staring at me weirdly" when she explained how their family day out would unfold.

Dutch courage came in the form of her cousin, who she bumped into despite a packed out stadium, and with her spirits up after this chance encounter, at half-time she began walking around the edge of the pitch trying to find a way to go in. The security guards were everywhere, so she prowled the perimeter like a lion looking for weak wildebeests amongst the herd.

"My plan was to find Richie McCaw and slap him on the bum," Rose told the *Daily Mail*. She eventually found a gap in the herd, and pegged it naked onto the field, with nothing on except for a hat and the word 'Kupa' in marker pen written across her back with the number 7. All Blacks coach Steve Hansen labelled her antics "a pain in the backside", which was not what Israel Dagg said, after she slapped

PILE ON

him on the bum instead of Richie McCaw, just as a Mexican wave went off around the stadium.

The crowd were cheering wildly as one of the security guards launched a flying tackle at her, landing the far side as she nimbly ducked under him. Not taking any chances on the second attempt, no fewer than eight of Napier's finest security guards surrounded her.

After quite a kerfuffle, Rose was removed to, "the back of a paddy wagon", where she waited for a couple hours. When she emerged, it was good news all round: the Kiwis had trounced Argentina 28-9 and Area Commander Inspector Tania Kura, who likes high horses, said that Ms Kupa met the criteria for a pre-charge warning only. "In this instance it was decided to issue Ms Kupa with a pre-charge warning due to the lower level of her offending, her attitude when arrested and the fact that she was sober. She was not deemed a risk for the rest of the night." and in a final flourish of officiousness "All cases are assessed on their merit and there is no standard charging process for streaking."

Rose told me in 2016, "Mum and Dad were proud, they were the first to call me. Such easy-going parents." She later reflected on her career as an army driver: "Some people have jobs to climb ladders at work, I have always had dreams of achieving fun things." She plans one day to get married in Vegas.

Another world-class bucket list entry, or excuse, came from Catherine Maher who ran across the field at the Brisbane Broncos vs Sydney Roosters rugby game, at the ANZ Stadium in Sydney, Australia in 2001. She wore nothing except two massive plastic pointy hands, held up to the sky. "It was something I wanted to do for myself," she told the court afterwards. "I have a list of things I want to do in life and that was one of them," she said. "This is the only way I can keep my sanity, what with being so involved with my children."

WHILE SHEILA NICHOLLS may have run onto the cricket pitch carrying a whole pile of baggage, thirty-three-year-old Jacqui Salmond (overleaf) "just really did it for the thrill of it".

THE ANATOMY OF
THE GOLF COURSE

Dropping your guard is hugely contagious. When one person sticks their neck out for a laugh, another will shortly follow. In Ray Stevens' number one record, 'The Streak', a witness to a streak asks his wife Ethel not to look, but it's too late. Later in the song the narrator sees the streaker again, but to his horror the streaker has been joined by his wife.

Contagion hit the Open in July 2000, where Jacqui found herself as one of no fewer than five streakers that day, although probably the person most likely to distract the players.

"I came up with the idea, for a bit of fun," she says. Seconds after Tiger Woods had teed off for the 18th hole, the mother of two hopped "over the front of the barriers" wearing a black dress "with no underwear on to make it easier". As she ran out, the black dress and everything else was quickly discarded except a pair of glasses, "purely because I couldn't see without them so I kept them on".

The Royal and Ancient Golf Club of St Andrews has never been known for its liberal values. Only in September 2014 did the club vote in favour of admitting female members onto a course that they consider to be the grandest in the world. For Jacqui however, it simply represented a stage. She just chose the championship because she "knew that lots of people were going to be there", and she wanted to feel the sensation of streaking.

As you can see from the photographs, in an unprecedented lust for life, Jacqui found herself facing a sea of police, spectators, cameramen and players advancing on her up the fairway as she gleefully "skipped round the flag a couple times" on the green. "I just wanted to run for the flag and run round it."

"I got taken to Cupar police station and it was quite funny because they actually put me in a white forensic suit because I had no clothes on, and I had to wear that until I got clothes the next day."

Tiger Woods went on to win at the Old Course that day, nineteen under par, the second triumph at a major championship in a month. The newspapers feared that Tiger was making golf too dull, and that he needed to give his rivals a chance. With a modicum of irony the R&A found itself simultaneously complaining about "switch-off factor" in golf, at the same time as streaking in golf.

A few months later, *19* magazine arranged for Jacqui, Mark Roberts and Erika Roe to meet in Manchester for a photoshoot. "We had drinks in the bar at the hotel comparing notes on what we did, it was fun. Mark Roberts – he's brilliant."

> ## "Then I went home and had a quiet time with the kids."
>
> Jacqui Salmond

Echoing other decisions she made at the time about her occupation as a dancer, the stay-at-home mum turned beauty therapist from Fife talked to me about the virtue of breaking free from convention, "It wasn't something I was ashamed of doing. If you want to do something like that, go for it, don't let anyone hold you back."

> ## "It just felt amazing, so out of the ordinary, a feeling never felt before, really ecstatic, really good."
>
> Jacqui Salmond

THE STREAKERS IN THIS CHAPTER express a similar sentiment to those in the first chapter in "not giving a nanosecond of consideration to the consequences", as Erika Roe put it, but in each it appears their silliness may have been, or become, a constructive moment in their lives.

"It's taken me a lot of time to figure out what the hell happened that day," Sheila tells me from her hundred year old Highland Park home, in a neighbourhood six miles from downtown LA. "What I know now, is that it was an explosion of this tightly wound collection of experiences and feelings, which had everything to do with pure rebellion," Sheila reflects on the desperate point in life she had reached, and her decision to destroy one reality in order to form a new one. She spoke about how that energy might have been channelled into other, more dangerous forms of rebellion, but was instead channeled it into something creative and fun, but also open to misinterpretation.

"I consider it to be a performance art, I consider it to be a feminist political action… People see a naked woman and immediately make it sexual and think it's about sexuality. It had nothing to do with that, even if it was a public event it was entirely about me, and entirely about choosing to be free."

> ## "It's not anything I'm ashamed of at all, it brought a bit of joy to the world."
>
> Sheila Nicholls

Streaking is a form of exhibitionism that has has a history of being distinguished apart from indecency or sexual motivation by judges, governments and medical authorities (see *Notes* for examples), due to the streaker's aim to have fun or to shock. Shortly after Sheila's streak, reporters from *Penthouse* would have been wise to make that distinction too, before they offered her a six-figure sum for a nude spread, in a conversation that would have been interesting to listen to. In fact, streaking itself has been used as a protest mechanism against sexualised nakedness, amongst other issues. In 1969 in Iowa, a spokesman from *Playboy* magazine attempted to give a talk on

'The Playboy Philosophy' to students at at Grinnell College. Female protesters took their clothes off in the audience, and when they demanded that he do the same, he fled.

In her cell in Paddington Green police station, Sheila sang to settle the other inmates. Eventually, she launched her own record label, Essex Girl Records, publishing on iTunes, writing songs for TV shows such as *Smallville*, and singing with her band Sheila and her Frocks, where she is currently working on "*All of Nature – a collection of social commentary to music*" and looking after a little girl. Sheila has had many accolades for her work as a singer-songwriter, not least her single 'Fallen For You', which was used on the soundtrack for the 2000 movie *High Fidelity*. Her appearance at Lord's is up there with her greatest hits. At 1.5 million views on YouTube to date, it is the most watched video of any of the streakers in this book.

Erika might not agree with me, considering her view that what she did was a spur of the moment decision, but for the streakers in this final chapter, I believe their moment in the spotlight was a way for them to say "*This is my life, this is who I am.*"

EPILOGUE

THE STREAKERS IN THIS BOOK are self-appointed legends of non-conformity and founders of a sport where the winners are the spectators. But most importantly, they are ordinary people having a bit of fun, and having spoken to many of them at length, it's easy to see that their respective moments *au naturel* changed their outlook on life forever. True, one of our streakers, Tim, didn't in fact make it, merely sliding down the ice rink wall like a starfish in a bottle, instantly knocking himself out. But all the interviewees state the importance of having their moments and exposing themselves, in both meanings of the word.

Constable Perry, whose use of a policeman's hat made Michael O'Brien's streak so internationally famous, saw the wider importance of his and Michael's moment as something that was actually important for society as a whole. The 1970s were a time of social upheaval; in the UK miners' strikes, electricity blackouts, the rise of Northern Irish terrorism and social division were heaping pressure on a police force rapidly losing morale. The photo at Twickenham humanised the police, and united all who saw it in the ultimate tool for social cohesion: laughter.

"There were a whole range of things the police were being knocked for at the time, and something like this had everybody smiling."

Constable Bruce Perry

Similarly, the wave of streakers across America in the 1970s lifted a nation's spirits while the US was still in shock from the Vietnam War, battle-worn by inflation and suffering pressure on wages and jobs. Where other forms of activism stoke tensions, the streakers in this book relieve them, combining influence with humour, while at the same time cheering people up in a world that, for the most part, takes itself very seriously indeed.

The importance of life's little diversions could not be overstated then and cannot be now. Every Friday during the summer of 2005, twenty-nine-year-old Andrea Hall ran naked down Tib Street in Manchester, for this very reason. "I felt so helpless after the London bombings and I just wanted to bring a smile to people's faces," she told the Manchester Evening News after expectant crowds started turning up each Friday. "There has been nothing else in the papers or on TV recently."

"When the world seems like it's going through a rough patch, the only thing I can do about it is to try to put a smile on people's faces."

Mark Roberts

Some of the streakers in this book created little moments of irreverence out of everyday life, some set out to delight audiences, and some found a deeper significance in their carefree moments. Like them, you can stand as naked as the day you were born on the bowls lawn in Hopton-on-Sea. You can skip through Lord's, leap across the Open, or dance into Twickenham. Or, if taking off your clothes in public happens to not be your thing, then throw caution to the wind and expose yourself another way, like writing a slightly eccentric book. For just one moment, you'll forget the rest of the world, and be witness to the transmissibility of joy.

I guess what I try to capture
and retain is that which you
see in very young children.
That glorious unselfconscious,
spontaneous freedom of
expression in being able to get
away with things."

Erika Roe

On 24 May 2006, Lakpa Tharke reached the summit of Mount Everest. He stood totally naked, for three whole minutes. Then, possibly with a todger resembling the bishop on a hand-carved miniature chess board, he pulled back on his climbing gear, attached and checked his oxygen supply, and successfully descended. Streakers instinctively know why it's important to let themselves go from time to time. This is a nod and a wink for anyone thinking of adding to the variety of life by losing themselves for a moment, taking a risk, and doing something a little bit different.

ACKNOWLEDGEMENTS

THIS BOOK would not have been possible without interviews and correspondence generously given by Tracy Mayhead, Missy Davies, Lianne Crofts, Erika Roe, Rose Kupa, Jacqui Salmond, Sheila Nicholls, Mark Roberts, Bruce McCauley, Christian Langford-Snape, Timothy Hurlbut, Michael Angelow, Bruce Perry, Professor Bill Kirkpatrick, and Professor Marvin Zuckerman. Thanks to each of you.

It would also not have been possible without encouragement and help from my wife, who was with me at Wimbledon when we stumbled upon a tennis match which quickly became the inspiration to write this book. Underdog Marcus Willis, the 772 ranked Downe House school tennis coach walked into Centre Court to face Roger Federer in the second round of Wimbledon 2016, where he spent 3 sets concentrating

169

hard on playing to the crowd, and much less so his opponent. Noted in the tennis world for Snickers and Coca-Cola court refreshments and sometimes forgetting his racquets, Willis was something of a sporting interloper himself, and the crowd loved him for it, rewarding him with several standing ovations. All of which was much more interesting than any tennis going on that day, and made me think that writing about this sort of shenanigans would be quite fun. It must have been tempting for her to suggest otherwise on many occasions since that match.

THE LAST WORD GOES TO THE
CAPTORS, IN THIS CASE A ROYAL
NAVY RESERVIST MILITARY
STEWARD AT WIMBLEDON, AND
MARK ROBERTS

Significant references:

Kirkpatrick, Bill. "'It Beats Rocks and Tear Gas': Streaking and Cultural Politics in the Post-Vietnam Era." *Journal of Popular Culture* 43, no. 5 (2010): 1023-1047.

"Streakerama: A Celebration of Streakers and Streaking." *Streakerama: The Streaking Site*. Last modified May 14, 2016. http://www.streakerama.com/.

"Streakers and Streaking." h2g2: *The Hitchhiker's Guide to the Galaxy: Earth Edition*. Last modified July 28, 2006. http://www.h2g2.com/entry/A7906872.

Introduction:

"A Look At UGA's History." *Welcome UGA*. Last modified August, 2016. http://welcome.uga.edu/UGAtimeline.html.

Bell, Thomas. "Nude Sherpa 'defiled' Everest to set record." *The Telegraph*, 27 May 2006.

Elliott, Keith. "The Sad Passing of the Naked Exhibitionist: Keith Elliott Charts the Rise and Demise of the Streakers." *Independent*. Last modified 29 August, 1994. http://www.independent.co.uk/voices/the-sad-passing-of-the-naked-

exhibitionist-keith-elliott-charts-the-rise-and-demise-of-the-
streakers-1386603.html.

Gasm Contributor. "Candy for the Naked Eye: Famous Streaking
Incidents of Yore." *Gasm.org*. Last modified September 10,
2014. http://gasm.org/article/candy-for-the-naked-eye-
streaking-incidents/.

Hoffman, Frank W. and William G. Bailey. *Sports & Recreation
Fads*. New York: Harrington Park Press, 1991.

The Mirror. March 7, 1974.

Wilson, Andrew. "From the Observer Archive, 17 March, 1974: the
naked truth about streaking." *The Guardian*. Last modified
March 22, 2015. https://www.theguardian.com/news/2015/
mar/22/naked-truth-about-seventies-streaking-craze.

CHAPTER ONE:

"10 weird and wonderful Wimbledon facts." *Staysure*. 21 June
2016. https://www.staysure.co.uk/2016/06/weird-and-
wonderful-wimbledon-facts/

"20 Instances of Streaker Invasions in Cricket." *NewsDog*.
Last modified 27 July, 2016. http://newsdog.today/a/
article/579894791290711ef73c790b/.

Bhattacharjee, Sayantan. "7 Incidents When Streakers Stole
the 1997 Masters Final streaker, X-rated, documentary
origin unknown, https://www.youtube.com/
watch?v=336Z5BhM7h0

Limelight." *Cricket Tracker Network*. Last modified October
28, 2015. http://www.crictracker.com/7-incidents-when-
streakers-stole-the-limelight/5/.

Charles, Chris. "Winning Streak Continues." *Fun and Games*. Last modified 22 April, 2004. http://news.bbc.co.uk/sport2/hi/funny_old_game/3648969.stm.

Daily Express. 8 July 1996.

Daily Express. 9 July 1996.

The Daily Telegraph. 11 February, 1997.

Eastern Daily Press. 19 January, 2000.

Edworthy, Sarah. "A day in the life: the grass." *Wimbledon*. Last modified July 5, 2015. http://www.wimbledon.com/en_GB/news/articles/2015-07-05/a_day_in_the_life_the_grass.html.

"Facts and Figures." *Wimbledon*. Accessed 14 November 2016. http://www.wimbledon.com/en_GB/atoz/faq_and_facts_and_figures.html

Harrison, Tracey and Lucy Turner. "Streaker Melissa Johnson; Strip Girl is Centre of Attraction." *The Mirror*, 8 July 1996.

Herald. 8 March, 2008.

Hockney, Karen. "Interview: Tracy Seargeant - Sorry, we didn't recognise you with your clothes on!; A one-off stripper and a serial streaker reveal what made them dare to bare all." *The Mirror*, 17 June 2000.

Kandohla, Tracey and Nick Parker. "Totty botty drives them potty." *The Sun*, 10 February, 1997.

"Marshall Takes His Chances to Book Quarter-final Place." *The Scotland Herald*. Last modified January 18, 2000. http://www.heraldscotland.com/news/12220876.Marshall_takes_his_chances_to_book_quarter_final_place/.

The Mirror. 17 June, 2000.

"Most Shocking Tennis Moments." *TennisNow*. Accessed November 14, 2016. http://www.tennisnow.com/MobileSite/BlogsDetails.aspx?BPostId=1970&BlogId=43.

Norwich Evening News. 19 January, 2000.

Oxlade, Andrea. "Pottering Around Norfolk: Back to the Old Days on a British Family Beach Break." *Daily Mail*, 15 November, 2011.

Rees, Paul. *When We Were Lions*. London: Aurum Press Ltd, 2016.

Streakers. Directed by Errol Morris. Originally released 2000. London: ZigZag Productions, 2000.

The Sumter Daily Item. 3 March, 1977.

The Sun. 19 January, 2000.

The Sunday Times. 20 October, 2002.

Sussman, Paul. "Winning Streak." *The Guardian*, 21 January 2000.

"Tracy Brings Bowls Bouncing into the Big Time." *The Sunday Times*, 23 January, 2000.

Whiting, Dan. *Characters of Cricket*. London: The History Press, 2015.

"Winning Streak at the World Indoor Bowls Championship." *publicfgures* (Tumblr Blog), 19 October 2012. http://publicfigures.tumblr.com/post/33892161508/winning-streak-at-the-world-indoor-bowls/embed.

CHAPTER TWO:

"20.04.72 Britain's First Streaker Meets His Match." *The Guardian*. Last modified 21 April, 2006. https://www.theguardian.com/sport/2006/apr/22/gdnsport3.sport.

Ashdown, John. "All Out at Lord's: Streaker Michael Angelow Paints Memorable Ashes on Scene." *The Guardian*, 2 August, 2016.

"Bates: Chelsea's Driving Force." *BBC Sport*. Last modified 2 July, 2003. http://news.bbc.co.uk/sport/hi/football/teams/c/chelsea/3037508.stm.

"Caption Competition 323." *BBC Sport*. Last modified 25 September, 2006. http://news.bbc.co.uk/sport2/hi/sports_talk/caption_comp/5379748.stm.

Daily Express. 6 August, 1975. 10 February, 1977.

The Independent. 25 July, 2004.

John. Emma. "Eddie 'the Eagle' Edwards is the loser who has a lesson for us all." *The Guardian*. 6 February 2016. https://www.theguardian.com/sport/blog/2016/feb/06/eddie-the-eagle-edwards-film-matthew-vaughn-biopic-winter-olympics-ski-jumper-calgary

"Lord's Streaker is a Hit for Twenty." *Glasgow Herald*, 6 August 1975.

The Mirror. 3 February, 2004.

"Quids Pro Quo." *The Age*, 6 August, 1975.

Romenesko, Jim. "Hockey streaker photo pulled after AP discovers manipulation." *Poynter*. Last modified 21 October, 2002. http://www.poynter.org/2002/hockey-streaker-photo-pulled-after-ap-discovers-manipulation/2891/.

The Streaker, Accessed 14 November 2016. http://www.thestreaker.org.uk/

"Streaker Ordered to Donate to Charity." *Huron Daily Tribune*. Last modified 26 April, 2016. http://www.michigansthumb. com/news/article/Streaker-Ordered-to-Donate-to-Charity-7373276.php.

The Sun. 6 August, 1975.

The Telegraph. 5 August, 1975.

Tinklin, Mark and Dirt. "Has a Streaker Ever Scored?" *The Guardian*, 6 July, 2005.

"Tom Spencer." *ESPN CricInfo*. Accessed 14 November, 2016. http://www.espncricinfo.com/england/content/player/20958. html.

Topping, Keith Telly. "The Fortysomethings' Guide to TV's Great Sporting Moments - A Second Extract." *From the North…* (blog). Last modified 24 January, 2009. http://keithtopping. blogspot.co.uk/2009/01/fortysomethings-guide-to-tvs-great_24.html.

"The Twickenham Streaker." *The Brother's Chronicle* 2, no. 10 (2013).

"The Twickenham Streaker." *Iconic Photos*. Last modified 30 July, 2007. https://iconicphotos.wordpress.com/2009/07/30/the-twickenham-streaker/.

Walton, Dawn. "Stamps Games Streakers Prove Too Cheeky for Management." *The Glove and Mail*. Last modified 14 March, 2009. http://www.theglobeandmail.com/news/national/stamps-games-streakers-prove-too-cheeky-for-management/article963656/.

"Where Are They Now?," *Channel 7 Australia*, 12th March 2006.

Chapter Three:

The Age. 11 January, 1982.

Daily Express. 30 May, 2015. 5 January, 1982.

Davies, Huw. *Another Weird Year: Bizarre News Stories from Around the World: Volume 1.* London: Ebury Press, 2002.

Donohoe, Graeme. "Streaker Jacqui Salmond Plots Revenge on Tiger Woods." *Scottish Sun,* 16 July, 2016.

"Erika Roe: The Twickenham Streaker." *Erika Roe.* Accessed 14 November 2016. http://www.erikaroe.com/

"Final Day for Streakers." *BBC Sport.* Last modified 24 July, 2000. http://news.bbc.co.uk/2/hi/uk_news/scotland/849101.stm.

"How Should We Tackle The Streakers?" *BBC Sport.* Last modified 7 August, 2000. http://news.bbc.co.uk/sport2/hi/sports_talk/869487.stm.

Lacey, Robert. *Great Tales from English History: The Truth About King Arthur, Lady Godiva, Richard the Lionheart, and More.* New York: Little, Brown and Company, 2004.

"Lap Dancer Fined for Tiger Kiss." *BBC Sport.* Last modified 23 December, 1999. http://news.bbc.co.uk/2/hi/uk_news/scotland/576469.stm.

The Mirror. 4 January, 1982. 5 January, 1982. 25 July, 1982.

Persaud, Joy. "Erika Roe: I Remember." *Reader's Digest.* Last modified 2016. http://www.readersdigest.co.uk/entertainment/celebrities/erika-roe-i-remember.

"Setting the boundaries: Reforming the law on sex offences." *Home Office.* April 2000. http://webarchive.nationalarchives.gov.uk/+/http://www.homeoffice.gov.uk/documents/vol1main.pdf

'Example judgements: ' R v Springer, 1975, Saskatchewan District Court and R v Niman, 1974, Ontario Provincial Court

Sheila Nicholls. Accessed 14 November 2016. http://sheilanicholls. com/

Smith, Leesa. "'A pain in the backside': All Blacks coach describing the cheeky moment woman streaked across field and slapped a star player on his rear end." *Daily Mail*. Last modified 8 September, 2014.

"Streaker!" Written by Bob Mills, Alastair Pirrie & Mick Hamilton, A Design for Television Production for Video Collection International, VHS 6463, 1995

The Sydney Morning Herald. 10 January, 1982.

Yates, Maria G. "15 of the Most Famous Streakers of All Time." *The Richest*. Last modified 5 August, 2014. http://www.therichest. com/buzz/15-of-the-most-famous-streakers-of-all-time/.

EPILOGUE:

BBC Sports Talk, Monday 7th August, 2000 https://www. theguardian.com/sport/2014/feb/04/reappraising-eddie- eagle-winter-olympics-ski-jumping

"Naked Ambition 'Kept Me Sane.'" *News24 Archives*. Accessed 14 November, 2016. http://www.news24.com/xArchive/Archive/ Naked-ambition-kept-me-sane-20010820.

"Uncovered - The Tib Street Streaker." *Manchester Evening News*. Last modified 12 January, 2013. http://www. manchestereveningnews.co.uk/news/greater-manchester- news/uncovered---the-tib-street-streaker-1077253.

Zuckerman, Marvin. *Sensation Seeking and Risky Behavior.* Washington, D.C.: American Psychological Association, 2007.

IMAGE CREDITS:

Usage rights for all images have been sought, and acknowledgement and thanks for the ones licenced go to: Alamy, Archant, Canadian Press, Getty, Ian Bradshaw, MirrorPix, PA Images, Rex, Shutterstock and Sportsphoto. A couple images are included as orphaned works or where contact was unsuccessful with the rights owner. Please reach out if you are the owner of these by emailing enquiries@ofdistinction.xyz. Finally, a few further images are included on the basis of permissibility as quotations of relevant work or broadcast, due to their already having been lawfully made available to the public by the rights holder, and the fact that usage in this book is as limited as it can be, with the purpose of quoting them solely for criticism and/or review of the streaker's performance and/or the photographer's work. In these cases, acknowledgement of the copyright holder is made on the image itself.